GOD'S

MASTERPIECE

By

JAMES WATSON

ISBN: 9798986087047

Editor
Teresa Hamilton
Doc Wilson
First printing edition 2022.

Publisher
Imagination Press, LLC
101 Cherry Lane
Glen Burnie, Maryland 21060
www.imaginationpress.website

DEDICATION

I would like to acknowledge My Lord and Savior Jesus Christ. Thank you for everything, even when I was hard headed and didn't listen you never turned your back on me. I appreciate you a lot.

Thanks to my best friend, Tiffany for always encouraging me to do better. Thank you Vanessa for always making me feel at home. Thank you Lee for all the nice haircuts, Thank you Jackie for coming to my shows and supporting a brother. Thank you Pumpkin, also known as Mom, for all your love. Thank you to my sister in poetry. Gwendolyn P. Smith for introducing me to Ms. Teresa Hamilton, my publisher. Gwendolyn, I really appreciate you to a lot.

TABLE OF CONTENTS

LETTER TO GOD

God I'm writing you this letter
Asking that you make things in my life a little bit better

I had some ups
And I had some downs

I had some smiles
And I had some frowns

I'm giving it my best
I thought I talk to you first Lord
Because I had some things I had to get off my chest

I need you to change my route
Because I'm stuck with no way out

I'm tired of running Lord
My legs are starting to get weak

I don't know what to say when I talk
Because my words will not come out right when I speak

I never meant to cause you any type of pain
I never meant to use your name in vain
Please forgive me if all I do is complain
I'm trying my best to hold on and maintain

But it's like I'm always caught up in the rain
Lord please accept my apology
I promise I will never do it again

I'M PREGNANT

Baby, I'm pregnant
Is it mine?

Whose else could it be
Please don't do this to me

I didn't create this on my own
This is what happens when we both decided to be grown

I'm not ready to be a dad
I'm still a young lad

And plus if I tell my parents
They are going to be mad

I thought you were on the pill
This is too much
How do you think I feel
I just need you to relax and chill
I know this all seems so unreal

I wish we could start over
But we're too late
Don't fly the coop now
I need you to step up to the plate

And be a man!

HAIRCUT

Next...

What can I do for you today
You can chop
A little bit off the top

How much do you want me to take off
Cut it down to a one
Okay I got you son

And can you go against the grain?
How about I give you a fade?
I would like that
And can you hit it with the blade

I got you!

How would you like me to do the back?
I like it round

How about I give you some design?
I like how that sounds

Okay here's the mirror
Man this looks good give me a pound!

HAUNTED HOUSE

I hear squeaking floors
And people slamming doors
I hear unusual sounds
And something moving around
These ghosts are starting to taunt me
These ghosts are starting to haunt me
I wish I could go back to sleep
But I can't
Because they're starting to give me the creeps
I'm starting to feel the fright
Now I believe them when they say
The freaks come out at night
I just want to run somewhere and hide
Because I'm feeling real shook up inside

DEMONS

I have demons I'm battling each and everyday
I get on my knees and pray
But they still will not go away
I never know when they're going to attack
And when I think they're gone
They keep on coming back
Oh God! Why can't I get these demons out of my heart
I just want to be free
But they're tearing me apart
They've gotten the best of me
I'm trying my best not to sin
But these demons are somehow controlling me from within
They know I'm weak when it comes to the flesh and the skin
I just want this torture to end
Before I spend
The rest of my life in hell!

TEN LAWS OF A WOMAN

The first law
To a woman's heart
Never break it apart

The second law
Don't look her in the eyes
If all you're going to do is tell her a lie

The third law
Whatever she says remember she's always right
And never argue with a woman because you'll never win that fight

The fourth law
If she's not happy you can't make her stay
And if you feel like you're going to put your hands on her just
walk away

The fifth law
Be sensitive to how she feels inside
Because there are some things she's not going to show you
Some things she's going to hide

The sixth law
Show her some respect
And never look at her as an object

The seventh law
Never accuse her
Use her
Or abuse her

The eighth law

If she's mad give her time to breathe
And if you feel like you're going to cheat on her just leave

The ninth law
Never aggravate her
Or frustrate her

And the tenth law
Always show her that you care for her
And that you'll always be there for her

AFRICA

This is the place of the motherland

A place where the world will never understand

There's some mystery here that have never been told

We're tropical people
We're not used to the cold
We come from a land of gold

And not from a land
Where people struggle everyday

We come from a land
Where people love to pray
We're not always living in poverty
We do own property
We started the whole ancestral vibe
We come from a background of strong tribes

You ever wonder why the hurricane always follows
the slave ships path
And why they're so devastating
Because that's God wrath
For those who treated us wrong
They should've kept us right where we belong
They always like to show people in Africa as being weak
But we're strong

SAME GOD

He's the very same God
Who said let there be light
He's the very same God
Who gave you the strength to fight
He's the very same God
Who told you not to give up
He's the very same God
Who will overflow your cup
He's the very same God
Who told you not to fear
He's the very same God
Who would wipe away all of your tears
He's the very same God
Who will turn things around
He's the very same God
Who will lift you up from the ground
He's the very same God
Who told you to get on your knees and pray
He's the very same God
Who will cast all your sins away

TIME MACHINE

I wish I could go back in time
And rearrange some things
I wish I could go back in time
And change some things

If I could
Do it all over again
I would

I wish I never made you cry
I wish I could turn back the hands of time
I would give it another try
But now it's too late

In time you build up so much hate
And you don't trust a word that I say
It's my fault why you're this way
If I could go back to that day
I would have pushed replay
And maybe everything would have been okay

They say in time you will heal
But the pain I caused you doesn't seem real
I understand how you feel
But why would you leave me
When I came this close to closing the deal

I wish I could go back into the past
But I can't
So I can only make what we have now last
I would have took my time
And not move so fast

JUSTICE SHALL BE SERVED

DEDICATED TO MAMIE TILL

I want the world to see what they've done
to my son!

He was wrongly accused, and physically abused

What they did to him, he didn't deserve and that's why I'm
fighting for justice to be served!

What they did to my son was a disgrace and that's why I want
them to see his face!

This was a violent crime against my son, and I thought it was time
for something to be done!

My son didn't deserve to die, and it all started because of a lie
I will not stop until someone pays for taking my son away
from me!

He would still be here today…

Now, I must live with the pain and make sure that
this doesn't happen again!

11

FREEDOM A POEM FOR JUNETEENTH

Freedom is being free
Freedom is no longer being in captivity
Freedom is being free to express your mind
Freedom is no longer being held behind
Freedom is standing up for what's right
Freedom is never giving up in a fight
Freedom is not being afraid to say what you want to say
Freedom is remembering those who paved the way
To get us where we are today
Freedom is for all the blood that we've shed
Freedom is for all the blood that we've bleed
Freedom is remembering all the sacrifices that our ancestors gave
It is up to us to no longer be a slave
That's what freedom is to me

WEDDING PLANS

I plan on making you my wife
I plan on being with you for the rest of my life

I'm sending out wedding invitations
For a very special occasion

Invite your family and friends
For a once in a life time event

Of sweet memories that will never end
Come share this special moment
With us

As we stand before Jesus
I just want this day to be perfect

All the hard work we put into it
It will all be worth it

I know you'll be happy once it's over and done
We might as well go all out
Because when it comes to life you only get one

And I just want this to be one day you will always think about

BELIEVE IN YOURSELF

No one believed in my dream
So I had to come up with a scheme
On how I was going to get this cream

With or without them
I was going to make it
Even if that means I have to take it

They told me I wouldn't go far
But God knew one day I would become a star

The same ones that didn't want to see me go far in life
Will be the same ones who will stab me in the back with a knife

I didn't lower my standards because of someone else
I believed in myself
Because at the end of the day
It only matters what God have to say

And I'm going to make it anyway
So I'm going to keep aiming for the sky
And tell them haters goodbye

WOLVES

Baltimore stay ganging up on people like a wolf pack
Anyone can be a prey for these streets when we attack
So if you don't want to get jumped you better watch your back
We a bunch of goons
Who stay howling at the moon
You're not messing with no coons
Over here
So when you see us coming
Stand clear
We put fear
In people's heart
And if you ever try to come against us
We'll tear you apart

HARD KNOCK LIFE

Some nights
We had no lights
We had to turn on the stove
Just to get some heat

Some days I opened the refrigerator
And there was nothing to eat

I'm scared to even get any sleep at night
Because I keep seeing a mouse
Running all through the house
Roaches running all in the cabinets
It just can't get
Anymore worse than this

I'm tired of eating oodles and noodles
I can't even afford to buy me a bag of cheese doodles

I'm down to my last cent
And I'm backed up on my rent

There's nothing left in my pocket but some lint
My paycheck isn't enough to get me by
And every night I just want to breakdown and cry

I can't even afford to buy me shoes for my feet
Everyday it's a struggle
Trying to get two ends to meet

RIVALS

He was the beast
From the east
And he was the best
In the west
Rivals in this game called rap
Both of these brothers were known across the map
Taken out by a gat
Did Pac snap
Or did he get caught up in a trap
Was Big innocent
Or was Pac jealous of his accomplishment
There's no telling how far these two brothers would have went
If they were alive today
It hurts me to my heart
To see two talented brothers taking away
It's Death Row verses Bad Boy
And they both gave us music that the world could enjoy
Was this gang related
Or was this case not properly investigated
Who was involved
Why wasn't this case ever solved
One wanted to dope slang
While the other wanted to gang bang
They say bullets have no name
And it's sad how these two brothers were taking out of the game

M.O.M.S. MOTHER'S OF MURDERED SONS

Why did my son
have to be the one

Who died by the hands of a gun

We're tired of the violence

We're tired of the nonsense

Something needs to happen
And it needs to happen now

Before another young man is gunned down
This needs attention worldwide
We can't keep pushing this to the side

We need to join hands
And make a stand

For what's right
Because we're losing the fight

No mother should have to go through
What we've been through
Because if it happened to us
It can happen to them too

We need to show unity
And give them an opportunity
We need to get these guns out of our community

We're trying to reach any council man governor or mayor
Because we need more than a solution

We need a prayer

BLACK MAN VS. A COP

It's a black man vs a cop
And when will the violence between the two stop
Black man stop showing us disrespect
And we will not look at you as a suspect
Black man if you don't want to be taking downtown
Stop hanging on the corners
If you don't want us to pat you down
Black man if you don't want us to pull out our gun
Please don't run
You're making it bad for everyone
Black man if you want to be treated fair
Don't reach in your pocket
Walk slowly to me with both your hands up in the air
Black man listen to my command
And if you don't cooperate
I will be forced to shoot you where you stand
Black man if you come at me with anger
I will shoot
Because now I feel like my life is in danger

MY LIFE

I can't be what you want me to be
I can only be me
Your life
And my life
Are not the same

So why do you get mad with me
Because I will not carrying out your name
I've been playing on your team
For a while
But I have my own dreams
My own style

I'm not trying to do what you do
I'm trying to be better than you
The sooner you get that through your head
The better off you'll be

Because this is my path that's being led
You can lead me to the water
But it's my choice to drink it or not
And this is my life in case you forgot

WE HAVE

We've been through the struggle
We've made it out of the jungle
We've been whipped on the outside
We've been stripped from our pride
We've never complained
We've took all of the pain
We've been used for so many years
We've been abused for so many years
We've made it out of the toughest situations
We've been held back from so many expectations
But we've kept on fighting for what's right
And never did we back down from a fight

HUG

Even a thug
Sometimes need a hug
It doesn't make you soft or sensitive
If more people could show you more love

This would be a better place to live
I know some people have you misunderstood
I know you're not always doing wrong
I know you want to do good
But you've been looked at this way for so long
It's hard to do right

So that's why you have your guards up
Ready to fight
People judge you
Before they get to know you
It makes it hard to trust anyone
But the Lord will show you
Who's really on your side
Or not

Some people don't mean you well
There's heaven on earth
Once you have gotten through the hell
A pat on the back is all you need
My brother I love you
And I want to see you succeed
So here's a hug

OL HAPPY DAYS

Bad days don't always last
This too shall pass
Good days
Are on their way
No more rain
No more pain
You can look forward to the sun again
Don't feel like this is a loss
Because you have so much to gain
Smile in your enemies face
Just when they thought you would be in last place
You've already won this race
No one can dim your light
Just like the stars at night
You will always shine bright
Too much for the human sight
Because they love when you do wrong
But hate when you do right

SOMEONE GREATER

There's someone greater
Than you and me

There's someone greater
Who will love you for eternity

There's someone greater
Who understands what you're going through

There's someone greater
Who will never turn his back on you

There's someone greater
Who will be there for you until the end

There's someone greater
Who you can call your friend

There's someone greater
Who will give you everything that you ask for

There's someone greater
Who will open and close all doors

There's someone greater
Who will never leave your side

There's someone greater
Who will always be there to provide

There's someone greater
Who will take away all of your fears

There's someone greater
Who will wipe away all of your tears
And that greater person is Jesus Christ

SEE YOU AGAIN

I miss you
I wish I can hug and kiss you
Life will never be the same
You will never be forgotten
We will always remember your
name
And what you stand for
My tears has fallen to the floor
As I look up at the sky
I can see heaven's door
As they open
I'm glad you're going to a better place
Even though my heart is forever broken
I hate the fact that we're apart
You will always have a place in my heart
When I look up in the sky
I hope to see you passing by
I want to cry so bad
But I know you don't want to see me like this
I just want to let you know
That you're truly miss
I love you so much
I would give anything just to feel your touch
I can't come with you on this ride
But one thing for sure
We'll see each other again on the other side

MEMORIAL DAY

Thank you to all the veterans on Memorial Day
Thank you for sacrificing your life
And paving the way

Thank you to all the recruits
We give you our highest salute

Thank you for keeping us in mind
When you're out there fighting behind enemies line

Your mission is never done
Until the battle is won

This goes out to those who are no longer here
We lay flowers on your grave

Thank you for all the hard fought battles
And being so brave
So long to all the soldiers
As we raised our hands and give you a wave

Thank you for our freedom
Because we could have been a slave

And because of your bravery
We're now saved

So we want to say thank you
For everything that you gave

STRESS KILLS

You're too blessed girl
To be this stressed girl
You need to leave him behind
He's making you lose your mind
And you don't need that in your life
You should be married somewhere being someone's wife
Why are you so stressed about him
You can do so much better without him
You need to breathe
Because he's sucking up all of your air
He has you so stressed
You started pulling out your hair
The way he treats you is so unfair
You really need to relax
Because he has you stressed out to the max
Never give someone that much power over you

AGREE TO DISAGREE

Girl why are you always giving me the third degree
What's the use of telling you anything
If all you're going to do is disagree

They say the truth shall set you free
I'm trying to come clean
I know you're upset
And you're saying things you don't really mean

I'm sorry baby
You said let me walk away before I say something I might regret
You said you will forgive me
But you will not forget

I never meant to hurt you
But you're not innocent
You did your dirt too
I just happened to get caught
And that's why every night we fought

How many times do I have to apologize
Until you realize
How bad you hurt me

YOU DESERVE IT

Mom today is your day
And you deserve all the good things coming your way
This is just a little appreciation for what you do
And I just want to tell you that I love you
Without you in my life
I wouldn't have made it this far
So on this day
You deserve to feel like a star

I hope what I wrote in this card puts a smile on your face
Mom thank you for all the times you kept me embraced
There will never be another who can take your place

I love you to the moon and back
Thank you for keeping me on track
I wish I could give you so much more
But all I can do is just bow down and give you an encore
There's no second guessing
You truly are a blessing

SHE'S NOT PERFECT

She's not perfect
But when it comes to her love
My baby is worth it
She may not be an angel from above
And that's okay
Because I love her anyway
Play with her emotions
And she'll break your heart
She comes with a little bit of commotion
But that's why she's such a work of art
You have to take the bad with the good
Some people have her misunderstood
I love her sassy attitude
And I don't mind her being a little bit rude
That's just how she operates
And that's what makes her the perfect soulmate

COME TO MY RESCUE

Lord my landlord wants to take me to court for rent
Lord I don't want them to put me out
And I have to live on the streets under a tent
I over spent
And I don't know where all of my money went

I'm sorry if I let you and my girlfriend down
I promise if you give me another chance
I'll turn this thing around
How could I jeopardize my livelihood
Thank God I have someone like you who's always good
I can't blame no one else
But myself

I'm the reason why we're in this situation in the first place
And when I told her how far we were behind
You should have seen her face
I ruined her birthday
And I know what I said

She didn't want to hear anything I had to say
I came too far to just give up now
And I don't care how much I'm behind
I will find a way to get this money down

MOUNT EVEREST

Many tried to climb Mount Everest
But could never finish their quest
Even they got tired trying
Or even they died trying
Some wouldn't stop
Until they've reached the top
Wind chill
Forty below zero
Maybe it's the thrill
Or maybe some wanted to feel like a hero
Some call it the mountain of death
Because it's enough to take your breath
Maybe it's the adrenaline you feel once you're up there
I don't know
Blistering cold and ground covered with snow
Many failed the test
Some will not rest
Until they've climbed Mount Everest
Then you can label yourself with the best
But until then
Try to conquer your quest

BLACK MAN STRUGGLE

They don't want a black man to receive education
They want us to be locked up for incarceration
They're trying to kill our kids
Wipe us out from the population
They don't want us to reach for the stars
They rather see us behind bars
Keep us blind with money clothes and cars
They're trying to poison our mind
Teach us about white man history
Keep us blind
Leave us in a mystery
They will not tell us the truth
That's why they're attacking our youth
With materialistic things
Because they fear one day we will become kings
They don't want us to uplift our brother
They want us to kill one another
That's why you see a lot of us in the hood
You don't see a lot of us in Hollywood
Because they think we're no good
And that we can't do what they do
But that isn't true

NOOSE

They hanging me by a noose
And they will not let me loose
It's like pick a nigger
Duck duck goose
Make sure that rope
Around his neck is tight
As my body starts to slope
I'm trying to hold on with all my might
But I'm running out of hope
This could be a horrible sight
If anyone sees me hanging here
I'm running low on air
I feel suffocated
And my pupils are dilated
The white man watch me as I dangle
I'm feeling pain from every angle
Trying not to strangle
As my body starts to mangle
Eyes rolling to the back of my head
A few seconds later I was pronounced dead

AM I ASHAMED

Am I ashamed
To walk in your grace
Am I ashamed
To look at your face
Am I ashamed
To say your name
Am I ashamed
To walk with the lame
Am I ashamed
To show you glory
Am I ashamed
To tell my story
Am I ashamed
To shed a few tears
Am I ashamed
To face my fears
Am I ashamed
To show you love
Am I ashamed
To look up to the sky above

CONDEMN ME

The devil wants to condemn me with guilt
He's trying to destroy everything that you built
He wants me to feel sorry for myself
But that's something I can't do
He wants me to love everyone else
Besides you
I make one mistake
The world hates me
But if they're going to hate
Let them hate
Because he didn't create me

I don't care if my enemy is trying to strike me
I don't care if my enemy doesn't like me
As long as I'm covered in your blood
I will not drown in the flood
He knows when I sin
He gets the win
But I rebuke that
In your Holy name
His love for me
And your love for me isn't the same

THE REASON WHY

Lord you're the reason why
I'm still here
Lord you're the reason why
I'm not going anywhere
Lord you're the reason why
I'm still standing
Lord you're the reason why
My wisdom is expanding
Lord you're the reason why
I have grace
Lord you're the reason why
I'm still in this race
Lord you're the reason why
I let go of my pride
Lord you're the reason why
I no longer have to hide
Lord you're the reason why
I get on my knees and pray
Lord you're the reason why
I'm able to see another day
Lord you're the reason why
I keep my head to the sky
Lord you're the reason why
I'm able to spread my wings and fly

I'M SAVED

I'm saved now
I'm not who I was before
You still want the old me around
But I said that person is no more
I was saved by grace
The old me has been replaced
To you it may feel kind of strange
But I had to change
I didn't do it for you
I did it for me
I had to do what I had to do
I got tired of who I used to be
You say that I'm acting different
You wonder where the old me went
I'm free from sin
This is where a new life for me begins

MY GIFT FROM GOD

My son
I gave you this gift
For you to use it to uplift
My people
Use it to your advantage
And I will give you the tools you need to
manage

I chose you over everyone else
I saw something in you
That I saw in myself
Your talent will take you very far
One day your talent will make you a star

I made you different
And the gift I blessed you with
Can only be heaven sent

Use this gift to bring me glory
Use the gift that I blessed you with to tell your story

SINS OF A FOOLISH MAN

I'm such a foolish man
I'm trying to avoid sinning
The best way that I can
But the devil is winning
And I'm losing all my grace
I feel like I'm in last place
And I'm losing this race
I already know what I'm doing isn't right
This battle between my mind and my heart
Is a battle I can't fight
My soul is falling apart
The more I sin
The further I'm away from the light
The person who is within
Is overshadowed by the night
I know if I continue to do this
It will cost me my life
Just like Judas betrayed you with a kiss
I got to let it go because it's not fair to my wife
That I keep holding on
And I know if you bless me
All my sins will be gone
I know this is a test for me
So I will not let it get the best of me

WHEN I THINK ABOUT YOU

When I think about you
I get goosebumps
When I think about you
My heart thumps
When I think about you
I can't stay still
When I think about you
I get the chills
When I think about you
There's a smile on my face
When I think about you
I'm filled with grace
When I think about you
I can't help but shout out your name
When I think about you
My life isn't the same
When I think about you
I feel blessed
When I think about you
I'm no longer stressed

HAPPY RETIREMENT

Happy retirement
We hate to see you go
These years went by so fast
No one thought that you would last
This long
But you proved them wrong
You been though all the ups and downs
Some days were easy
And some days were hard
But you still stuck around
So dedicated
And so motivated
You let nothing hold you back
You made a positive impact
To your crew and team
And we wish you the best
On all your accomplishments and dreams
We knew this time would come one day
We just hate to see you go
But we know you must be on your way
Enjoy this time to yourself
Because we know you have given so much to everyone else
You will definitely be missed
At least you have time to think about all the good times
Cherish the moment
As you enjoy your retirement

DREAMS

Is it an illusion

Am I stuck in a delusion

Is it fake

Or is it real

Because I don't want to awake

From something I can only reveal

When I'm deep

In my sleep

Do dreams come true

When I'm daydreaming

Do I even have a clue

Is it a mirage

Or is it a fantasy

Because if I'm sleeping peacefully

Please don't awake me

MARRIED TO THE GAME

I'm married to the game
I've done gave the streets my last name
For better or for worse
I will always put these streets first
I've done made these streets my wife
I've done gave these streets half of my life
Forever we will be
Until the day they bury you and me
I will never leave your side
The rest of my life with you I'm willing to spend
Because not only are you my bride
But my best friend
And I will always be down to ride
With you until the very end

MY GUITAR

It's just me and my guitar
One day it's going to make me a star
You play the melody
And I will sing
Together we make such beautiful harmony
When I pluck you by the string
Every time we hit the stage
It's like we're on the same page
You know exactly what the crowd likes to hear
You create such a beautiful sound
So loud and clear
Acoustic
Or electric
Rock and roll
Or soul

A WORD WITH SATAN

Satan what is it that you want?

Your soul

You can't have it

Are you telling me no

Yes

See you want me to lie down in my mess

You don't care nothing about me

To you I will always be worthless

So why must I confess

My sins to you

When I can confess them to the one who makes me feel blessed

You're nothing but stress

And you always make me feel depressed

I don't want to listen to a word you have to say

Because all it's going to do is make me walk away

I will not let you ruin my day

Before I do that

I will just get on my knees and pray

TIME

It's time for me to move on
One thing we can't get back is time
Once it's gone
It's gone
Time stops for no one
Once your time is done
You're done
You don't have time for me
I don't have time for you
You hurt me one to many times
Multiply that times two
They say in time we'll heal
But how is that possible
When time stands still
You will not give me the time of the day
And that's the reason why our precious time
Has gone away

MISSION IMPOSSIBLE

My mission is to make you smile
My mission is to walk you down that aisle
But that would be impossible if you've haven't done it in a while
My mission is to make you my wife
My mission is to give you a better life
But that would be impossible if you're used to living in strife
My mission is to make sure that you succeed
My mission is to give you anything that you need
But that would be impossible if you never been given
satisfaction guaranteed
My mission is to take care of your heart
My mission is to make sure that no one breaks it apart
But that would be impossible if you never been given
a brand new start
My mission is to make you my bride
My mission is to never leave your side
But that would be impossible if you don't let go of your pride
My mission is to lift some of these burdens off your chest
My mission is to give you my very best
But that would be impossible if you're not willing to go
with me on this quest

PRECIOUS NAME OF JESUS CHRIST

Heavenly Father thank you for the death of your son
Because he died for me
My battle was already won
He put his own life on the line
Just to make sure I was fine
He took my pain
So I wouldn't have to feel it again
And for that I will never complain
Or ever use his name in vain
I wouldn't be here
If it wasn't for him
He paved the way
No one knows the price he had to pay
In order for us to stay
On earth another day
But because he took our place
We now have grace

MY FATHER'S WILL

All I was trying to do is get my father's word fulfilled

But they wanted me killed

Why did they want an innocent man like me blood spilled

If it weren't for me they would have died in their sins

But since my father loved them so much

They get to see his blessing from within

They beat me

And hung me to my death

They forgot that I was the one that gave them breath

I was supposed to die

So they may live

And even though they did this to me

For them I will forgive

KEEP ON GOING

Keep on going
And never stop
Keep on going
Until you've reached the top
Keep on going
Even when life seems to keep you down
Keep on going
God will turn things around
Keep on going
Everything will be alright
Keep on going
You've already won the fight
Keep on going
You're almost there
Keep on going
You can make it anywhere
I don't know who needs to hear this today
But I'm telling you to keep on going
And let nothing get in your way

FIRST TIME I MET YOU

The first time I met you
I just knew I wanted to be with you for the rest of my life
The first time I met you
I just knew I had to make you my wife
The first time I met you
I never knew I would fall this deep in love
The first time I met you
I never knew I would receive an angel from above
The first time I met you
I never knew I would find my best friend
The first time I met you
I never knew all my heart ache would come to an end
The first time I met you
You took my breath away
The first time I met you
I was speechless with nothing to say
I just had to make you mine
The first time I met you
Where there was a dark space now the sun shines

STAR

I think you're taking your problems a little bit too far

You shouldn't have to when you know that you're a star

You're the light

makes the sky shine at night

you the sky can't shine as bright

So make a wish

I'm so proud of all the things you accomplish

When your stars align

You can see your true zodiac sign

When the sky is clear

That's when you appear

Twinkle twinkle little star

How I wonder how far you are

SORRY FOR YOUR LOSS

Sorry for your loss
Remember in time of grief
Look to the cross
He will give you a bit of relief
My condolences goes out to you
No one really knows what you're going through
Dealing with death is really hard
That's why when death comes about
The only person we can really turn to is God
He will find you a way out
I know all you want to do now is cry
And I don't blame you
Because if something like this happened to me
I would probably do the same to
It's okay to feel a little down
It's okay to want to show a frown
I know it hurts you to your heart
Seeing someone that you love so much depart

DUMB AND DUMBER

How could I be so dumb
To let you tear me apart
How could I be so dumb
To let you continue to break my heart
I played your fool
And that's cool
Yes you played with my mind
I was so blind
I couldn't see the signs
How could I be so stupid
To not see that you hid
This right under my eyelids
I should've caught on
When you said you don't want a woman with kids
My heart got in the way

DETECTIVE

I'm looking for any trace or clues
I'm checking this place for residue
I'm looking for hints
Or any type of fingerprints
I'm going to take you down to the station
So we can do a little investigation
I have a warrant to search the place
I don't have a lot of time
I must solve this crime
In 48 hours or it will be considered a cold case
Never in history
Have we had an unsolved mystery
I'm not trying to prosecute you
I just want to take you to the interrogation room
for a quick interview
I call in the forensic team
To check the scene
The truth shall be revealed
And I'm not stopping
Until this case is sealed

HELP IS ON THE WAY

Help is on the way
So just hang in there just a little bit longer
What don't kill you will only make you stronger
Don't throw in the towel just yet
Things will get better
No matter how hard things may get
God knows what you're going through
And I'm telling you that He hasn't left you
Just when you feel like you're about to give up
And throw it all in
That's when you're about to win
If you can withstand the bruises and the scars
God will put you on top of the world
Like the sun moon and the stars
God knows you can't do it alone
And he knows you can't do it on your own
Don't be afraid to ask him for a helping hand
That's what he's here for
To help you stand

ONE MOMENT IN TIME

I will succeed
Even when you think I'm not
I'm coming for the number one spot
It's mine guaranteed
I'm going to give it all I got
Even if it causes me to bleed

I will fight
With all of my might
I'm breaking down all barriers and walls
I'm standing tall
Through it all
Victory is mine
This is my time to shine

I'm making moves
Because I got something to prove
I will not let nothing mess up my groove

Until I've reached the top

Then that's when I will stop
I'm in my prime

When it's all said and done
I will be remembered as the greatest of all time
Because everyone remembers number one
No one remembers number two

TORNADO

Something spiraling down from the sky
Destroying everything that comes by

When you touchdown
It only takes minutes
For you to destroy a whole town

They call you the devil's tail
You bring lightning and hail

You cause so much destruction
In the radius of a mile wide
The safest thing for you to do
Is to run and hide

I will try not to get caught up in your path
Because I don't want to be taking for a ride

Dust
Winds
And debris
Knocking down buildings and trees
When you see one coming at you
What will you do

LAUGH NOW CRY LATER

They laughed at me
Told me that I was ugly
They tried to ruin my pride
I was too afraid to smile
So I use to cover my mouth
Ashamed of who I was on the outside
Kids used to stare in my face
They never seen someone's teeth look so out of place
So I would run and hide
Just to avoid them
Because I didn't want any problems
I didn't let what they say
Ruin my day
I still walked with my head held high
To the sky
They tried to hurt me down to the core
But all it did was made me love myself even more

GOOD MORNING BEAUTIFUL

It's always good when you hear someone say
How beautiful you look today
A compliment can go a long way
People will try to destroy your pride
But you should never hide
From whom you are inside

No matter how much people try to tear you down
Pick yourself up off the ground
And never let them see you frown
You should always love yourself
No matter what anyone else
Has to say

And just like the sun shines above
That's how you should feel each and everyday
You should always feel like you are being
loved
And thought of in each and every way

B.E.T.
BLACK ENTERTAINMENT TELEVISION

I bet
You regret
The day you let
A white man take over your set

You might as well change your name
To W.E.T
Which stands for White Entertainment Television
Because you lost your vision
When you decide to make that decision

Your sitcoms
Were sold to a bunch of redneck Uncle Toms
What **were you** thinking about
Now you're known for being a sellout

You used to be for the culture
But you gave it up **to** a bunch of vultures

VIOLATION

It's no fun being violated
What he did to you left you devastated
You tried to tell someone about the situation
But they thought you was trying to ruin his reputation
He said if you tell anyone
You're done
What else could you do
If no one is believing in you
He took your dignity
He took your pride
He took your virginity
He destroyed everything who you was inside
You hate yourself because of what he did
But it's not your fault
You were just being a kid
Now you keep your feelings locked in a vault
He made you hate all men
And that's why you could never trust another man ever again

THE G.O.A.T

They call me the G.O.A.T.
Which means that I'm the greatest of all time
No one could mess with me when I was in my prime
I've been in this game for a while
Many tried to duplicate my style
But I'm one of a kind
Talent like this is hard to find
When I'm long gone
They're still going to remember my name
I'm a legend in the game
Without me in it
It's not the same
It will not be long before I make it into the hall of fame
When I do it I do it with heart
I'm crushing all of my competitors
When it comes to my art
No one can do it better

SHARE YOU WITH NO ONE ELSE

Baby I'm not sharing you with no one else
I want you all to myself
Call me selfish
But I don't care
Call me stingy
But I don't like to share
I just can't see you with another person
If it's not with me
Can't you see
We were meant to be
I can't see no one else up in that
It's going to hurt my pride
I can't see you with no one else
If it's not me by your side
I'm telling you now
There's no place you rather be
Because no one else is going to put it down
Like me
No one going to do
The things I do to you
Like I can
If you think the grass is greener on the other side
Go right ahead
That person will never be me
You're going to wish you were with me instead

IT'S NOT A RACE

It's not a race
Missing with me you'll end up in last place
Before you cross the finish line
Think twice about messing with mine
You're in no position
To be messing with someone who's nowhere close to my
competition
I will run laps all over you
I'm leaving my competitors in the dust
And there's not to many people in this game that I trust
Some try to catch up with me
But still can't adjust
To my flow
Like the wind I'm blowing right pass them
See everyone out for my trophy Because they know I'm a problem
Before you step on the field
Make sure you're protected with your sword and shield

HOW DO YOU FORGIVE

How do you forgive those who hurt you
How do you forgive those who desert you
How do you forgive those who cheat on you
How do you forgive those who beat on you
How do you forgive those who hate you
How do you forgive those who violate you
How do you forgive those who steals from you
How do you forgive those who squeals on you
How do you forgive those who calls you out your name
How do you forgive those who always accusing you for the blame
How do you forgive those who make you cry
How do you forgive those who tell you a lie
How do you forgive those who been accusing you of doing
something wrong
How do you forgive those who been using you for so long
Forgiving someone is the hard part
But if you decide to forgive someone it should be from the heart

THE FALL OF THE TWIN TOWERS

This looks like something from a movie
But this wasn't no movie
This was reality
I thought I was dreaming
But when I saw them planes run right into the buildings
I started screaming
This can't be happening right now
Then a few minutes later
The towers came tumbling down
All I can do was pray
And hope that everyone was okay
No one will ever forget what happened on this day
So many Americans lives were taken away
I can't imagine the pain that they've felt
It just makes my heart melt
I am deeply hurt to the core
It was the most horrifying thing I have ever seen before
My heart will forever be sore
I don't think I will ever be the same anymore
My heart goes out to the family Of the victims
who are no longer here
May God bless you
And keep you in good care

ONE WORD TO DESCRIBE YOU

One word to describe you
Brilliant
Magnificent
Intelligent
Excellent
Elegant
Gorgeous
Outrageous
Marvelous
Precious
Courageous
Beautiful
Wonderful
Thankful
Grateful
Insightful
Delightful
Positive
Sensitive
Appealing
Revealing
Emotional
Devotional
These are the words that describe you!

GIRL POWER

Don't be fooled
Girls may be as delicate as a flower
But they have enough power
To bring down the strongest tower
They just want to be treated the same
And not be called out their name
Because when a girl is on fire
Watch out
Because she is coming to take over the empire
And there's nothing no man can do about
One day a girl
Is going to rule the world
And every man will have to bow down
And give up his crown
To the Queen
By any means
A girl is our backbone
And God knew a man couldn't do it alone
That's why he created a woman

ROCKET SCIENCE

Baby this isn't rocket science
This is common sense
Was there something I miss
Because I can't see why you're having a hard time with this
Stop over working your brain
This is so simple and plain
What are you stressing about
If you don't get it by now
You're never going to figure it out
You're no fool
You did graduate from school
Did you
This is elementary
And should be as easy as ABC
123

A SPECIAL CEREMONY

We're getting married
Together in holy matrimony
This is a celebration
A special ceremony
Together we will be
For eternity
As we join hands
And stand
Before the preacher
Family and friends fill the bleachers
I can't help but to smile
As I see you coming down the aisle
I've been waiting for this day for a while
And now the day is finally here
Now that I got you where I want you
You're not going anywhere
So as your father hands you away
In my heart you will always have a place to stay
I'm nervous as hell right now
But in my mind I know it's about to go down
This is the happiest day of my life
That day when I became your husband
And you became my wife

MOONLIGHT

Moonlight moonlight
Oh how beautiful you glow at night
With a light
That shines so bright
You're such a beautiful sight
And I just want to wrap my arms around you
and squeeze you tight
A great big round ball in the sky that glow
With a light that is as white as snow
Why are you so far away
And why the only time I see you is at night
Do you sleep during the day
I can't look at the sun for too long
I'm afraid of going blind
But when I look at you
Everything is fine
I just want to wrap my lasso around you
And pull you down from the sky above
Sing to you
As I spread my love

CELEBRATE YOUR LIFE

Your life we celebrate
As you exit the earth on that special day
This is your expiration date
As your soul is lifted and carried away
You will be truly miss
Your life we shall reminisce
And even though I'm sad
I must remember
That the good will outweigh the bad
We shall not mourn the fact that you're gone
But we shall be happy that you're moving on
To a place
Where your soul shall be place
And filled with the Lord's grace
No longer do you have to suffer in vain
And no more do you have to feel pain
And if it's meant to be
We shall see each other again

STAGE FRIGHT

I can't let the audience get to me
I can't let them see me sweat
I have to go out there and give them a good show
No matter how loud they may get
I don't want to choke
Because if I do
They may take me as a joke
Even though I'm nervous
I'll be fine
Because I was made for this
And it's my time to shine
I will not fear the spotlight
I will be okay once I get pass my stage fright

PENS AND NEEDLES

The pen is my needle
I take the needle and pierce my skin
As the pen bleeds from within
My soul
I can't let this high go
Writing down my pain
The adrenaline going through my vein
Making it hard for me to cope
I'm losing all sense of hope
Strung out on dope
My eyes are blood shot red
And rolling to the back of my head
Body filled with led
I look like a zombie half dead
Can you see what I'm thinking
My eyes will not stop blinking
I could write a book
On how I was so hook on drugs
Would you open it up and take a look
Or would you sweep it under a rug

ALLEN IVERSON THE ANSWER

Allen Iverson made a name for himself
He wasn't the same as everyone else
Coming from the project
And small town in Newport
Allen Iverson gained his respect
On and off the court
His kind was very rare
Tattooed down with cornrows in his hair
He played with an attitude
And because of that
People thought his presence was rude
But he was just spitting facts
Allen Iverson always been a competitor
He had his own style
And was so versatile
One simple fight
That happened at midnight
At a bowling alley
Started a big rally
It almost ended his career
He was charged with twenty years
Then a second chance came around
And he joined the University of Georgetown
He left college early to play
In the NBA
He was an ankle breaker
And a risk taker
And one of the league's best play maker
They don't call him the answer for no reason
He won rookie of the year his first season
He influenced the mind of other
And that's why there will never be another

COLD WORLD

It's a cold world
Baby girl
You got pregnant at an early age
Working your but off everyday
Just to receive minimum wage
Can't go home because all your parents do is fight
And you can't get no sleep at night
Looking for attention
But the only way these boys will look
Is if your clothes are tight
You're in college
But can't afford to pay for your books
You smoke cigarettes one time
And now you're hook
All you need is a little support
But you can't even get that
It seems like the world is against you
And no one has your back
You've been abused
And used
By man
And now you don't know who to trust
They tell you they love you
But it's only lust
You tried to slit your wrist many of times
You pop pills just to ease your mind
And you don't want no one feeling sorry for you
Because of what you're going through
Just pray for me
You tell them
Because one day
God is going to take away all of your problems

MONEY BAG

I'm trying to get this money bag
So fresh and so clean
Without the soap and rag
No slacking
I'm stacking
And racking
This money up
So what's cracking
Because when it comes to the bag
I'm never lacking
Money is the only thing that I care about
And if I were to ever run out
I'll just go out there and get some more
Because as long as I got money
I will never be broke or poor

UBER EATS

Hi

My name is Jay

I'll be your driver for today

Place your order

And once you've done that

I'll be on my way

If I take a while

You can always check my profile

I always give good service

With a smile

I'll make sure your food is on time and hot

Rate me five stars

I would appreciate it a lot

You can leave a tip behind

If you don't mind

WELCOME TO BALTIMORE

Welcome to Baltimore
Where every year the death toll continues to rise
Over three hundred murders
Don't be surprised
If you see someone you know on the news
City infected with rats roaches and mouse
Neighborhoods filled with vacant houses
Everybody knows everyone
So watch who you talk to
Don't get caught sleeping or you're done
Be careful who's neighborhood you walk through
Syringes on the ground
Chesapeake full of bodies that have never been found
Pit bull fights
And kids riding dirt bikes
Stickup kids robbing you in broad daylight
City filled with crooked cops
Everywhere you go
You see yellow, red and blue tops
Crackheads high off methanol
Homeless people panhandling for drugs and alcohol

NEVER DOUBT YOURSELF

Never doubt yourself
Never lower your standards because of someone else

You do have what it takes to go far
Keep reaching for the stars

All you have to do is believe
And you will achieve

Always strive to be your best
Put yourself above all the rest

One day you will make it
Whatever you want
Just go out there and take it

It's your turn to shine
Let nothing stop you from crossing that finish line

You will win this race
And you will be in first place
No matter how hard the obstacles you may have to face

YOUR UNDERSTANDING

Why do we blame God
When someone's life is taking away
When we know that no one lives forever
That we all have to go someday
God gave us grief
To be a sign of relief
But we're so caught up in our feelings
That we show him disbelief
We should not disrespect God's authorities
Because we're caught up in our own priorities
God has been around longer then we have
So let's show him some seniority
Because he's the God of immorality
As a man
We may never understand
God's plan

LIBERTY

They say it's liberty and justices for all
But lately I watch our liberty and justices fall
Our country is in shambles
Full of propaganda and scandals
The real one that committed the crime
Are getting away free
While the innocent man is doing time
And being treated unfairly
I don't put my trust in politicians
Or these coalitions
Because they have no intuitions
They're all crooked in my eyes
Full of deceitfulness and lies
The way they run this jurisdictions system isn't right
And one day it's going to come to the light

MY MOM

Mom even though you were never around
I thank you for keeping my feet on solid ground
Mom I miss your warm kisses and hugs
Mom I still don't understand
Why you chose to use drugs
I wish I were there to give you a helping hand
Mom I don't think you know what your death has done to me
I don't have an ounce of love left in my body
Mom I never understood
Why you and dad used to fight
Mom I hate when you wasn't home
To tuck me in the bed at night
Mom because of you
I struggled in relationships
I didn't have you there to give me any tips
I didn't have you there to teach me the game
And because of that
I treated all females the same
Instead of me treating them like a queen
They were just something I wanted to get in between

COMING TO HER AIDE

I want to put her on a stretcher
While I will take her body and stretch her I told her to relax and
let me take her vital signs
Her blood pressure is out of line
How do you feel right now
Do you need to lay down
Are you a diabetic
Or are you an asthmatic
It I didn't reach her in time
Things could have gotten worse
Are you sure you don't need to see a nurse
Let me rush her to the hospital and quick
Because she looks very sick
I think she need to go to the emergency room right away
Don't you let it go by another day

PARANOIA

I think people are out to get me
I can't control my anxiety
I'm losing my mind
But if I stay on my meds
I should be fine
These voices are messing with my head
I find it hard to stand still
And I'm down to my last pill
Now I have to go to the pharmacy to get a refill
People say that I need to just chill
And I look at them and say
That's easy for you to say
You don't have to feel what I'm going through everyday
I wish I can make it go away
But it always comes back
And I hate the feeling like I'm being attacked

HAPPY THANKSGIVING

I thank God for all the things I was giving
I thank God for the life I'm living
So as we bow our heads and say our grace
Thank you for allowing us to sit at the table
As we feed our face
Thank you for gathering us in one place
Turkey
Stuffing
Macaroni and cheese
And yams
Collard greens
Cranberry sauce
Sauerkraut
And ham
I don't care if my tummy hurts
There's always room for some desert
Gobble
I ate so much food
Now I'm starting to wobble wobble
Later on if I'm in the mood
I think I will give my family a call
See if they want to come over and watch a game of football
Then after the game
We going shopping for Black Friday sales at the mall

CONTROL

I don't want to lose control
But it seems like I'm locked up
Doing life behind bars with no parole
I thought I would be fine
But I find myself crossing the line
Every single time
I didn't know loving you would be a crime
I noticed when it comes to you
I can't control the things I do
Trying to hold my composure
Baby this is pure torture
And I just need some kind of closure
I don't need the exposure
Sometimes I have to control myself
Before I zap out on someone else
I'm getting too old for this
I'm too old to be this upset

SEPARATED 2

Baby we're separated
I just want us to make it
But you said that you couldn't tolerated
So I found someone else who would take it
You said you can't take this another day
That it hurts more if you stay
You said it would be better if we part ways
Baby how could this be
I thought you were the one for me
You said what we had is gone
That you're ready to move on
I said if you do this you'll regret it
And you looked at me and said
I don't think you get it
What we had is no more
I said baby are you sure
You know we've been down this road before
You said yes
And you replied
That you can't deal with the stress

I CRY

I cry
For all the victims who died in the hands of a police man
I cry
For those who fought hard to make a stand
I cry
For those who lost their life to Covid
I cry
For those who are innocent and in jail doing a life bid
I cry
For those who ever lost someone they truly love
I cry
For those who ever had to fight just to stay above
I cry
For those who ever had their heart broken
I cry
For those who are looking for the truth but been outspoken
I cry
For the mothers who give birth
I cry
For those who don't know how much they are worth
I cry
For those who are struggling everyday just to survive
I cry
For those who are out there busting their tails working two nine
to five
I cry
For those who ever been abused
I cry
For those who ever been used

MARIO'S WORLD

I can hear your heart
Crying out for me
And it's dying for me to set it free
Baby how do I breathe
Knowing he's tearing you apart
What is it going to be
Him or me
Baby there's no right and wrong way
To how you feel about this
But if you decide to stay
You will regret it everyday
He's not a one woman's man
Baby you have too many options
To walk away
I promise if you let me love you
You'll see that I'm here to stay
How could you let him
Put his hands on you
You deserve so much more than what you're going through
Why didn't you call the cops
C'mon baby use your head
If this nonsense doesn't stop
I'm afraid they're going to find you somewhere dead
See I care for you
And that's not what lovers do
See I'm just a friend
Who cares about what you're going through
See you just need some protection
And someone to guide you in the right direction
Baby you just need someone to show you a little bit of affection
So don't be afraid to look into the mirror
Because what you'll see is your true reflection

Adapted from songs produced by Mario Dewar Barrett

ASK IN MY NAME

Ask in my name
And you shall receive
No one will ever love you the same
This I believe
Don't be afraid to ask me for anything when you pray
If I don't give it to you right away
It will come another day
Remember
Patience is a virtue
And I already heard everything you had to say
You may not be ready for what I'm about to give you
It's going to be overwhelming
It may leave you a little stressed
But if you can handle it
Then you will truly be blessed

HAVE MERCY ON ME

I was just trying to show you who my father was from within
That if you believe in me
You'll be forgiven for your sins
But you took nails and pierced my skin
You spit on me
And you hit me with stones
Even though my cross was heavy
I showed not one weakness in my bones
I didn't look at you with shame
But asked my father to forgive you in my name
Because I know you're not the one to blame
And even though you did this to me
I will still love you the same
This how much I love you
That I would put no one above you
Tell me
Who would do this for someone they've never seen before
This is what I'm willing to give plus more

LEAVE IT UP TO YOU

Baby I'm going to leave it up to you
So tell me what do you want to do
Because I can't do this anymore
I'm just tired of my heart feeling sore
Let me be straight forward and upfront
With you
I think we need more time to think about what we want
To do
If it was up to me
I would have walked away
But since I left it up to you
You probably wanted to stay
It's too late
To try and make this work
It's too late
To try and erase the hurt
What's done is done
I wouldn't wish this on anyone

WOULD YOU STILL LOVE ME

Would you still love me
If I made you cry
Would you still love me
If I told you a lie
Would you still love me
If I wasn't perfect
Would you still love me
If I wasn't worth it
Would you still love me
If I told you I didn't love you
Would you still love me
If I put someone above you
Would you still love me
If we got into a fight
Would you still love me
If I didn't treat you right
Would you still love me
If I broke your heart
Would you still love me
Till death do us part
Would you still love me
Because this is where my heart needs to be
With you

HOLY NAME

Lord I'm calling on your holy name
You said
Once I come into your life
You will never be the same
I'm the healer
And the revealer
I'm the Lord of all creation
And the only one who can bring you to salvation
No man
Will ever love you like I can
All I ask is that you believe
Trust in me
And you shall receive
Love me with your whole heart
And I promise never to break it apart
I will find you a way
When you think there's no way out
The best thing for you to do is to pray
When you start to have doubts
I will never turn away your hand
If there's something you don't know
I will help you to understand
My love comes without fear
And I will not put more on you that you can bare
I will pore you out a blessing from the heavens above
And I will do this just to show you my love

PLAYING THE VICTIM

I hate when people always playing the victim
Always want you to feel sorry for them
Everything in their life is always going wrong
Their stories are long
And their always giving you this sad song
They always complaining about dumb stuff
You're not the only person that has it rough
Get over it
Brush yourself off
Because I don't want to hear it
If you're not going to do something about the situation
Keep quit
I'm tired of hearing about your problems
So stop telling me
Because I don't have the answer to solve any of them

PUNCHING BAG

Please tell me girl
Is it true
That he left your eye
Black and blue
I just don't have a clue
Why you let someone do this to you
Put away them boxing glove
Because I know you're tired of being pounded on love
He hit you so hard
Like he was Mike Tyson
And you were Evander Holyfield
I wish I were there to block all them punches
Because baby I don't mind being your shield
I know you're tired of going round for round
Pound for pound
With him
You wish someone would stop this fight
But he hit you with a left
And a right
Pow!!!
You're down for the count

DAVID AND GOLIATH

No matter how big my problems may get
And no matter the size of my opponent
I will fight
With all my might
I will not let it defeat me
Nor will I let it beat me
I'm not intimidated
Because of your height
And if you come to me with a problem
I will knock you down with one strike
Because there's no fear in me
And I will not back down
No matter what the situation may be

YOU LOVE ME STILL

You love me still
Even when I didn't trust in your will
And when I went astray
And didn't listen to a word you had to say
You never turned me away
Because you knew I would need you one day
Even when I was covered in sin
And lust for the skin
You still love me from within
Even when I was full of pride
And pushed you to the side
Still you provide

CAN WE GET ALONG

Baby why can't we get along
What was it that I've done
That was so wrong
I apologize
I didn't realize
It would hurt you this way
So I don't blame you if you decide not to stay
This is the price I'm going to have to pay
I can apologize a million times
But if you don't accept one
Then what I'm apologizing for really doesn't matter
Why would someone throw a brick
At a heart made of glass
Just to watch it shatter
How disrespectful could I be
Wasn't thinking about your feelings
I was selfish and only thinking about me
It caused me the most precious thing in the world
And that was you girl
If I could go back in time
And change anything I would
I would take all the bad days
And replace them with the good
I know you can't stand to look at me right now
And I don't blame you
Because if that was me
I would have done the same too

LONELY

Baby sometimes it can get cold at night
That's when I'll be there to hold you tight
You'll never have to sleep alone
As long as I'm home
This bed was made for two
Never will you wake up
And not seeing me lying next to you
The only thing keeping you company is your pillow
Staring out your window
Hoping that I come through
But I don't
Looking at my picture on your dresser
You can't take the pressure
Anymore
You get a knock at your door
It was me
Thank God you came over
I got tired of being lonely

CAN'T AFFORD TO LOSE YOU

I can't afford
To lose you Lord
Without you I'm nothing
I'm tired of suffering
I can't make it on my own
Let your presence be known
Please give me the wisdom and knowledge to know
Please give me the strength and length to grow
Lord I will not give up without a fight
Lord I don't want to do it
If it's not pleasing to your sight
Lord I don't want to do it
If it's not right
Lord I'm tired of living in darkness
Lord I need your light

MAYBE NOT

Should we tie the knot
Maybe not
She's all I got
Maybe not
She's so hot
Maybe not
I love her a lot
Maybe not
When I found her I hit the jackpot
Maybe not
Should I give her a shot
Maybe not
She's far from a thot
Maybe not

HIDE AND GO SEEK

Baby let's play a little game of hide and go seek
Close your eyes and count to ten
And please don't peek
I bet you can't find me
Now where could you be
Am I getting cold
Or am I getting hot
I don't know where you're at
You hide in the perfect spot
This game taking longer than I thought
I'm about to give up
But as soon as I done that
That's when you was about to get caught
Now I'm chasing you all around
The playground
The only reason why you were found
Was because you made a sound

MY FIRST GRANDCHILD

You're my first grandchild
And I'm going to show you all my love
God has blessed me with an angel from above
I will protect you with all of my heart
No one will ever tear us apart
Anything you need from me
I will be there to provide
All you have to do is just call
And I will be right by your side
To catch you when you fall
I can't wait to see your beautiful face
I can't wait to hold you in my arms
And keep you embrace
Don't be alarmed
Where there's danger
Grandma will keep you away from harm
I can't wait until you start to talk
I can't wait until you start to walk
We're going to go everywhere
Shopping and more
I can't wait until we go get our feet and nails done
At the spa store
I'm going to shout out loud
And let everyone know how proud
I am to be your grandma

BOO THANG

I do it all for you
You're my boo
No matter what we've been through
I know you'll have my back
That's why I don't mind spending a couple of stacks
On you
Some nights
We fight
But I'm the first person you call
When you want to be held tight
Plus you know if you want to hit the mall
You know I'm going to keep you looking right
You're my superwoman
I'm your kryptonite
When my stomach was starving for something to eat
You cure my appetite
Girl you're fine
But don't get it twisted
When another woman get out of line
She doesn't mind
Letting another woman know that she's mine
When I'm out there being on my grind
I know she'll be right there
Because when I need her
She's not too far behind
Plus she knows when I get this money
Half of it hers
That's why I love my boo
Because she's one of a kind
I can't see how another man would treat her wrong
Because ever since I met her
Our love been strong

WOULD YOU BE MY VALENTINE

Baby would you be my Valentine
Because darn you're fine
Let me take you out
Let me show you what this day is all about
When Cupid shot his dart
I didn't have a clue it would lead me right to your heart
Here's some edible underwear
Chocolates
Balloons
And a teddy bear
I hope this put a smile on your face
But wait
We're not done yet
Dinner for two at my place
This will be a day that you will never forget
Why chose one day
To show you how much I care
When I can show you
365 days out of the year

NO MAKEUP

Baby you don't have to put on any makeup
Just to please me
You look just as beautiful when you wake up
So don't cover up your beauty
I think you're more finer
Without all that eye shadow and eye liner
You're more distinguish
Without all that blemish
Stop hiding yourself from the world
And let everyone see that beautiful face girl
All that makeup doesn't make you more beautiful
It just makes you more insecure

I WANT YOU BACK

There will never be another man who will love you
The way I do

They're only there for a season
I'm here for a reason

Stop listening to everyone and what they say about me
And trust in your heart
Because as far as I see
They're just trying to keep us apart

Trust and believe
Anything I ask God for
I will receive

What did I do that was so wrong
That made you just want to move on

Anything worth having
Is worth fighting for

One day I will have you back in my life
One day I will make you my wife

I'm going to give you some time to get over yourself
By that time I hope you don't find someone else

I will never stop loving you
Until the day I die
And that's no lie

You bring out the best in me
And if it's truly meant to be
It will come back around
And if it doesn't
Then I wish you the best
I had to tell you this
Because it was on my chest
I will always love you
No matter who you're with
You will always be my most precious gift

LAST WORDS BEFORE I DIE

I know you're wondering why
I chose the streets
I know you're wondering why
I'm lying under these sheets
But your dad chose the wrong path
And baby girl
I wish I can tell you all the things I did
But I can only tell you half
And some things you will not understand
Because you're only a kid
And this is the aftermath
Of all the things I hid
From you as a child
Yes your dad was running the streets and acting wild
I was up to no good
If I could take back all the things I've done
I would
Never thought I would die in the hands of someone gun
But this is the price you pay
When you're living that life
Now I won't be able to see that day
When you get married and become someone's wife
How selfish could I be
To not see
How much you meant to me
But now it's too late
And I don't want you to grow up with hate
In your heart
Because me and you are apart
All I can say is that I'm sorry
But don't you worry
Because if I make it to that special place
We'll see each other again
So keep a smile on your face

RUN BLACK MAN RUN

Run black man run
The war against you isn't done
The war against you just begun
Run black man run
And don't you stop
Because once you do
That's when their guns go pop
Run black man run
Before they gun you down in these streets
You don't have a place in this world
You'll always be beneath the white man's feet
Run black man run
Until your feet start to hurt
Keep on running before they put you in the dirt
Run black man run
Because once you do
That could be the end of you
So run black man run
Before you become a victim of another one

DIAMONDS

Girl like a diamond you shine
Girl like a diamond you're so fine
Like a diamond in the rough
Girl when it comes to your love
I just can't get enough
Girl like a diamond
I'm your best friend
And like a diamond
Forever we will be
Until the very end
How can something made from coal
Bring together two souls
Because once you're mine
I'm never letting go

HEY DAD

Hey dad I have a birthday coming up in a couple of days
And I was wondering if you could come by
I know you and mommy parted ways
And until this day I still don't know why
But I really miss you
Sometimes I wish I could hug and kiss you
I haven't seen you in so long
And I was wondering did I do something wrong
Because I feel like it's my fault that you and mommy are not
together anymore
I just wish things were like they were before
Before all the fussing
And the cussing
I hate to see you and mommy fight over me
It's just not right you see
That day the two of you split apart
It really broke my heart
I hated the both of you that day
And you wonder why I act a certain way
Some things I don't talk about
I just wish you and mommy somehow work it out
I'm tired of being teased at school
And the way you and mommy keep fighting isn't cool
I don't think the both of you know what you're doing to me
I wish the two of you makeup and just let it be

IF I DIDN'T CARE

Baby if I didn't care
Why would I still
Pay all of your bills
Baby if I didn't care
Why would I let you walk away
Instead of making you stay
Baby if I didn't care
Why would I let you be happy with someone else
Instead of myself
Baby if I didn't care
Why would I waste my time arguing with you
And why would I let you do what you want to do
Baby if I didn't care
Why would I let you have the keys to my place
And why would I let you have your personal space
So you can't say I don't care about you
When I do

R.A.C.E
RESPECT ALL COLORS AND
ETHNICITIES

We're all the same
The only thing that makes us different
Is probably our name
God loved all of us
Black, white yellow or brown
So let's lift one another up
And stop putting each other down
The color of our skin
Shouldn't define who we are from within
Let's not pretend
That racism doesn't exist
It's our choice to put it to an end
And it's up to us
To come together and mend
Even though we're a different kind of blend

NOT THE ANSWER

War is not the answer
We have more battles to think about
Like aids and cancer
No more blood shed
No more people ending up dead
We need to end this revolution
And come up with a better solution
Too much money being spent on weapons of mass destruction
We need to spend this money on reproduction
And infrastructure
So let's end this massacre
No more war in the Middle East
So let's increase the peace

QUEEN ELIZABETH II
LONG LIVE THE QUEEN

Long live the Queen
The most polite and respectful person the world has ever seen
She came from great royalty
And showed everyone in Great Britain loyalty
There will never be another who can take her place
She put a smile on so many people face
The world is in shock right now
Who else is going to wear her crown
She showed the world so much love
And she was truly an angel from above
We will never forget her name
Britain will never be the same
A true monarch
With a great heart
An icon
Your legacy will forever live on
Even though you're gone
Rest in power
As the people of London cover your memorial with flowers
We honor the most high
As the world says goodbye
To the Queen

REFLECTIONS OF A QUEEN

When you look in the mirror
You will see a reflection of a queen
The most beautiful woman
The world has ever seen
You're his clone
He can't do it alone
He needs a queen like you to run his throne
He needs someone like you who can be his backbone
He needs someone like you who can hold him down
Someone who has enough power to wear his crown
You're his majesty
His empress
His higher authority
His highness
He needs someone like you who can show him loyalty
He needs someone like you who can give him royalty
He needs someone like you to have his back
He needs someone like you to pick up his slack
When he has falling off track

ALWAYS AND FOREVER

Always and forever
You will always be in my heart
Always and forever
Until death do us part
Always and forever
I will always be there
Always and forever
I'm not going anywhere
Always and forever
I will always put you first
Always and forever
We will always be together for better or for worse
Always and forever
I will not stop until I've made you my bride
Always and forever
We will always be side by side
Always and forever
Until the day I say I do
Always and forever
I will always love you

TIME TO REST

It's time for you to rest
You have finished your quest
When it comes to life
You have given it your best
You may now sleep in peace
For your soul has been released
To the heavens
No more suffering
No more pain
Brighter days are coming
And the sun will shine again
Even after the rain
When you awaken
You will be in paradise
For your soul has been taken
To the other side
This has been one hell of a ride
So sleep
And may the Lord keep
You in his arms forevermore

HUSSLE HARD
DEDICATED TO NIPSEY HUSSLE

You grind hard each and every day
It's sad how your life was taken away
This was your final victory lap
Now it's time for you to take your eternal nap
You were going to make a change
How your life was taken away
It all seems so strange
Maybe you knew something we didn't know
Or maybe the world wasn't ready for what you were about to show
Your life was taken away too soon
This all seems so unrealistic
As if it was a cartoon
That you were taken away by some knucklehead goon
You encourage many to strive
You were going to change lives
On how to survive
In these streets
They feared your mind
They feared your grind
You had a vision
So to take you out
Was their only decision
They didn't want you to succeed
So they rather see you bleed
The world will never be the same
You taught us how to play the game
And never let the game play you
We will never forget your name
So long my friend
Until we meet again

SATAN'S BETRAYAL

Satan was the most beautiful angel in heaven
He had the most beautiful face
But he still wasn't satisfied
He wanted to take God's place
So God kicked him out of heaven
Satan was giving his own empire
And it was called hell
A place where there was darkness and fire
A place where those who sin would dwell
Satan will give you all the riches you desire
And that's how man gets caught up in his spell
He doesn't tell you that you will spend your entire
Life in a cell
Satan can never give you joy
All he wants to do is kill steal and destroy
He knows that he only has a short period of time left
That's why he's always on the attack
Because he knows that the Lord is coming back

PLASTIC SURGERY

You got butt injection
Now you're suffering from an infection
Silicone in your breast
You thought it would make you look good
But it makes you look a total mess
Trying to look like them girls in Hollywood
Botox in your lips
And in your hips
Why are you trying to look like everyone else
Do you love yourself
Because I don't think you do
Draw on eyebrows
Every time you look in the mirror
You ask yourself who what when where and how
You're trying your best
To try and fit in with the rest
You must be sick in your mind
If you think this is going to make you look fine
Either you're dumb death or blind
Or maybe you don't see the sign
They're not going to tell you the truth about plastic surgery
They just want your money

YOU DON'T KNOW
WHAT I'VE BEEN THROUGH

You don't know what I've been through
And if you did
Would you be able to walk in my shoes
I've been abused and I've been hurt
I've been through the trenches
And I've been through the dirt
My trials and tribulations
Have taken over my situations
But now I have a revelation
On how God brought me to salvation
Many tried to judge me
But they could never budge me
So before you look at me or someone else
Take a good look at yourself
You're no better than me or them
And you will see that we all have the same problem
No one knows all the tears I've cried
No one knows how hard I've tried
Everyone has their own story to tell
It's not in his plan for me to fail
When people try to put me in a shell
God said one day I shall prevail

TOSSING AND TURNING

Girl I'm tossing and turning in my bed
And it's interrupting my sleep at night
I can't seem to get you out my head
Something just doesn't seem right
You got me taking sleeping pills
And I'm waking up in the middle of the night with cold chills
I got it bad
I wish we would have made up before I went to sleep
Because I hate going to bed mad
I feel restless
Girl can you see I'm stressed
I feel a total mess
I got to go to work in the morning
My eyes are heavy
But all I've been doing is yawning
Sleeping without you in this bed is boring
If I'm not sleepy
Why am I snoring

LIP GLOSS

I love when you put on your lip gloss
I love when you take your tongue
And lick them across
It makes your lips look so fine
And it gives your lips a little bit of shine
There's something about your lip balm
That drives a man like me crazy
But I must remain calm
And try not to let it faze me
It makes your lips look ten times better
And it makes your lips look ten times wetter
I can't help myself
I just want to give you a kiss
I don't know about everyone else
But when I see them lips I can't resist

I AM NOT A NIGGER

I am not a nigger
Who you think is rude
I am not a nigger
Who you think has an attitude
But a black man who should be shown some gratitude
I am not a nigger
Who you think is ignorant
I am not a nigger
Who you think is arrogant
But a black man that's intelligent
I am not a nigger
Who you think is uneducated
I am not a nigger
Who likes to stay incarcerated
But a black man who will not be tolerated
I am not a nigger
Who you think is a thug
I am not a nigger
Who likes to sell drugs
But a black man who just needs a hug

PLANTATION

Pick that cotton nigger
You filthy rotten nigger
I don't care how long you've been out here
You're not going anywhere
I don't care how much your hands hurt
Get back to work
No break for you today
Keep picking that cotton nigger
Or else you will pay
But master I'm weak
And I haven't had nothing to eat
It's hot out here
And I'm about to rot out here
What you're giving me lip nigger
Take your shirt off
And take this whip nigger

MOMENT OF SILENCE

I would like to take a moment of silence
To those who lost their life due to violence
We must stop killing one another
And show love to our sister and brother
Something must be done
And it needs to happen now
Before another one
Be shot down
A change must start here
If we want to get somewhere
We must fight
For what's right
Give one another an opportunity
If we want to see a change in our community
We can't hide from this anymore
We must dig down deep to the core
I must not be blind to the fact
That this thing doesn't have an impact
On us
Because it does
I'm taking a moment of silence one time for the decease
Let's stop the killing and increase the peace

WHITE CHOCOLATE

They want to talk like us
They want to walk like us
They want to listen to rap like us
Hang in the trap like us
But until you've been enslaved like us
You could never be us
Until you've been beaten and misbehaved like us
You could never be us
They try to cook like us
Even try to look like us
Wear their hair like us
Be on welfare like us
But until you've felt our pain
Been abused slaughtered and slain
You will never be us

DO RIGHT

Mom I know you were trying your best to do right
But your addiction was too hard for you to fight

No one knew what you had to face
If only they were in your place

Only God knows your pain

While everyone else's days were full of sunshine
Yours was filled with nothing but rain

You had no one to turn to
All they did was judge you
When they should've had your back
But they did not
So you turned to crack

Because it was the only thing you had at the time
When you were going through a lot
I don't know why until this day
Why you chose drugs over your family
And we may never understand I just wish we could have been
there to give you a helping hand

IN YOUR HANDS

Lord I just don't understand
Don't worry my son
No matter what
Your life is in my hands

But Lord if that's the case
How come I can't see your face
Just because you can't see my face
Doesn't mean I'm not there
I'm just like the air
You can't see me
But you can feel my presence

Lord I want to believe
But the devil is making me deceive
And that's why I can't receive your blessing
Lord I'm just tired of stressing
My life is in shambles
And I feel like a chicken with its head cut off
Running around trying to scramble
Around my problems
That's why I'm having this talk with you
Because I don't know who else can solve them
Indeed I will help you to succeed
Thanks for trusting in me
In your time of need

I PLEDGE ALLEGIANCE TO THE FLAG
THE STAR SPANGLED BANNER

I pledge allegiance to the flag
Why are my black men keep ending up in a body bag
In America
And to the republic from which it stands
The police can't keep their hands
Off our black men
One nation under God
Living in a white America is so hard
With liberty and justice for all
This country just wants to see our black men fall

The star spangled banner

Oh say can you see
My people just want to be free
By the dawn early nights
Our people just want to be treated fair
And have equal rights
What so proudly we hailed
In their eyes we've already failed
At the twilight's last gleaming
As you whip us
Can you hear us screaming
Who's brought stripes and bright stars
The blood we wipe from our bruises and scars
Through the perilous fight
What they did to us wasn't right
O'er the ramparts we watched
Were so gallantly streaming
To be free in America

I was only dreaming

And the rockets' red glare
Living in America is a nightmare
The bombs bursting in air
My people just want to be treated fair
Gave proof to the night
They just want to kill us on sight
That our flag was still there
The white man don't really want us here
O say does that star spangled banner yet wave
O'er the land of the free
They will keep hanging us by a tree
And the home of the brave
We will always be a slave

THE FLAG

What does this flag really represent
It doesn't represent me
If so then our people would be free
The national anthem
Represent colonialism
And racism
The red
Is for the blood my people shed
The blue
Is for the things they don't want us to pursue
And the stars
Are for the scars
They left on our back
Because to be black
In America is a crime
This is more than a rhyme
This is a resolution
For the revolution

POOR LEADERSHIP

Brandon Scott
You say you're stopping crime
But you're not
Because every day in Baltimore city
People are still being shot
You talk a good game
Accusing everyone else for your poor decision
When really you're the one to blame
How can you sleep at night
Knowing that you're dragging people along
We need someone who can do the job right
We need a leader that's strong
You're too weak
And you will not look at the camera when you speak
I can look you right in your eyes
And see that you're telling us a bunch of lies
We need someone with good leadership
We need someone who is wise
Because with you in office
The murder rate will continue to rise

COLLECTION PLATE

People use the collection plate to manipulate people
People use the collection plate to bait people
You're supposed to be giving to God
But you're giving it to them
And that's where I have a problem
It's supposed to be a donation
But they're using it for their own situations
It's all smiles when they pass that collection plate round
But as soon as you don't give they frown
Bribing people
And conniving people
With their shenanigans
I wish they stop jiving people
Taking people money
Like it's funny
What's the real reason why you want our money
Stop playing us for a dummy
Because we're not falling for it
Now take that to your pulpit

FOLLOW YOUR DREAMS

Follow your dream
Even though others may seem
Like what you're doing isn't right
Some may not agree with your decision
And that's okay
Because they don't have God's vision
They don't understand his ways
Whatever God set out for you is for you
All you have to do is trust in him
And he will see you through
He will not leave you stranded
Or abandoned
He will always be by your side
No matter what
He will provide
Follow him
And he will be your guide
So follow your heart
And you will see the blessing that God start
To bring in your life

FEEL BEAUTIFUL

Beauty is in the eyes of the beholder
So you got every right to walk around with a chip
on your shoulder
You're beautiful no matter what anyone has to say
Remember God made you different in his own unique way
When you look at yourself in the mirror everyday
You should encourage yourself
And say I love you
Even if you don't hear it from anyone else
You should always feel blessed
Because God don't make no mess

SISTERHOOD

We have a bond that no one can break
Whatever I have to do
However long it's going to take
I'm going to make sure you're straight
You'll always be my sister as long as I live
No one can compare to the love that you give
I will always have your back
And I will always be there for you
No matter where you're at
We have a relationship that no one can tear apart
You will always be the closest thing to my heart
What we've built
Someone would try to destroy
I love being around you
It brings me so much joy
You're my sister forever
No matter what we will always be together

LION KING

I'm the King of the jungle
Always ready to attack
Ferocious and furious
Amongst the pack
They don't call me the King
For nothing
Terror and fear is what I bring
I'll rip you with my claws
And crush you with my jaws
My roar
Is something you just can't ignore
My family I will protect
In the jungle
Everyone shows me respect

DEATH

One day we will all meet death
One day we will all take that final breath
Death is promised to us all
One day we will all get that call
Will you be ready when it comes knocking at your door
Because nothing can prepare you for what's in store
Does death means that we're really done
Or is there another life after this one
We will all be buried six feet deep
As we lay on our back
We will take that eternal sleep
As our eyes will be forever close
And we will see nothing but black
As our body rots and decompose
Death is taken very hard
And sometimes death is always blamed on God
Death is a relief
Not a grief
And when it comes to death
People have different beliefs

GOOD LUCK

Farewell my friend
Your journey has come to an end
We will always remember your name
Never forget how far you've came
Whoever comes after you will have a lot of shoes to fill
Enjoy this time off to relax and chill

We know you can't be with us forever
We know you're off to something so much better
Thank you for the time we've spent together
It was truly worth the while
We will never forget your wonderful attitude
And your beautiful smile
You were a blessing to everyone you've touched
And we will miss you very much
Good luck on all of your accomplishments
You are truly magnificent

I WILL RETURN

Take what you have learn
I haven't left you
One day I will return
But for now
Look to the sky above
I will be looking down
Guiding you every step of the way
It wasn't meant for me to stay
I will rise in three days
Don't you worry
And don't you fret
Never forget
What I told you
When you need some comfort
I will be there to hold you
When you need some support
I will be there to mold you
No one will know when
But until then
Live your life
Because I'm coming back for my wife

MY BEGOTTEN SON

I can conquer all things
I even took all of the suffering
You nailed my hands and feet
You thought that I was weak
You even pierced my side
To see if I died
As you helplessly look at me and cried
I came into this world to save you
From the evil that tries to enslave you
I was the gift my Father above gave you
It was in his will
That my blood be spilled
In order for the scriptures to be fulfilled
Through my scars you will be healed
My love for you is unlike any other
That any man can give
I was sent into this world to die for you
So that you may live
If my Father didn't love you
He wouldn't have given up his only begotten Son
But he sacrificed my life
So that you and He could be one

THE FINAL HOUR

Jesus you told them all along
What they did to you that was wrong
But you forgave them
And held on strong

Your own people wanted you punished
Your soul they diminish
As you look down and told them it was finish

No one believed you
When you told them that you were coming back
The sky started to turn black
As the ground started to crack

The ground started to rumble
As the Roman temple started to crumble
The Roman guards started to stumble
But your people remain humble

Because they knew that the time has arrived

PEARLY GATES

There's a long wait
To get through the pearly gate

Everyone will have their time and date
When God will decide your fate

So change your ways before it's too late

How you live down here
Will determine how you live up there

Heaven is more beautiful than it looks
Everyone wants their name to be written down in that book

Will you be one of the ones
God looks to and says well done

Everyone wants to make it to that special place
Everyone wants a chance to see the Lord's face

But not everyone will get that chance to feel the Lord's grace

There's a long line ahead
Are you willing to wait
To make it through the pearly gate

WELL DONE

I can't wait until that day comes
When he says to me well done
You have made it in my son
The most precious words
That any man has ever heard
All of your good deeds will not get you in
But what will get you in
If you repent for all of your sins
It's an honor to see your face
It's an honor to feel your grace
And it will be an honor to be accepted into your place
Don't feel bad if he neglects you
Don't feel bad if he rejects you
Everyone can't come
Only some

To book James Watson for your next conference or in-house event, please contact him at poetryemotion2012@gmail.com.

ORGANIZATIONS and CORPORATIONS

This book is available at special quantity discounts for bulk purchases. This book is perfect for employee gifts, sales promotions, premiums, or fund-raising. Give the gift of God's Masterpiece!